The Hidden Heart Series
"Self-Esteem"

Copyright © 2014 by Cindy Dahl
All rights reserved
www.cindydahl2007.wordpress.com

Art by Shaun Crum

ISBN-13: 978-1-941030-07-3

SELF-ESTEEM

By Cindy Dahl

Illustrated By Shaun Crum

Hi, I am a GLíCK. You say it like /glēk/.
It stands for Giving, Loving, Inspiring, Caring and Kind. My books will show you how to be a GLíCK just like me!
I have hidden a heart in one of the pages; see if you can find the love in this book.

Hint: The hidden heart is near balloons.

Just saying kind words
Like, "I think you're sweet,"
Makes you feel good
And gives others a treat.

You might be good
At catching frogs or bugs.
Or maybe you are good
At giving big, huge hugs.

Stop! Think of something
That you do really well.
Maybe you have
An amazing story to tell.

Some people are funny
And really make us laugh.
We might chuckle so hard
That we bend in half.

There are still others
Who are really good at art.
Maybe putting things together,
Then taking them apart.

Nobody is perfect,
So put that out of your mind.
We may not be perfect,
But we're all one-of-a-kind.

So, say it out loud,
My name is "_____."
And what I am good at is,
"_____."

That's right, you are special,
And you should be proud.
It makes it so real
When you say it out loud.

Share this with friends.
Tell them they're good too.
This will help their self esteem
Just like you!

"You yourself, as much as anybody
in the entire universe, deserve YOUR
love and affection"

— *Gautama Buddha*

Cindy Dahl is the author of several feel good children's books including the entire "hidden heart series" where kids get to find the hidden heart in each book. "It's like finding the love in the pages of a book." Cindy's main goal with writing her books is to inspire and bring a positive message for kids at a very young age. "It is never too young to learn to be kind to one another, to feel good about yourself, and to share with others."

Cindy grew up on a farm in Northern California and currently resides in Colorado. Cindy has three grown children. She read to them often when they were young and loved watching their faces when they felt the story come alive. In her spare time, Cindy enjoys being in the great Colorado outdoors.

www.ingramcontent.com/pod-product-compliance
Lightning Source LLC
Chambersburg PA
CBHW040017050426
42451CB00002B/19